# *Small Colleges*
# BIG MISSIONS

---

COMMISSION ON SMALL AND/OR
RURAL COMMUNITY COLLEGES

---

American Association of Community Colleges

---

W.A. Griffin, Jr., *Editor*

© Copyright 1995 The American Association of Community Colleges

**Printed in the U.S.A.**

All rights reserved. No part of this book may be reproduced or transmitted in any form or by any means, electronic or mechanical, including photocopying, recording, or by any information storage and retrieval system, without written permission from the publisher.

Published by the
American Association of Community Colleges
National Center for Higher Education
One Dupont Circle, NW, Suite 410
Washington, DC 20036-1176
202/728-0200

Manuscipt Editors: Bob Greiner and Ron Stanley
Design: Maryam Makhzani
Cover Design: Gehle Design
Printing: Good Printers

**ISBN 0-87117-285-2**

# TABLE OF CONTENTS

1993-1994 Members of the American Association of Community College's Commission on Small and/or Rural Community Colleges ........................................................ v

Introduction ............................................................................................ vii
*by W.A. Griffin, Jr.*

| | | |
|---|---|---|
| Chapter 1 | Leaders Through Community Service .......................... 1 *by Jacqueline D. Taylor* | |
| Chapter 2 | The Role of Institutional Research ........................... 11 *by Ford Craig and W.A. Griffin, Jr.* | |
| Chapter 3 | Small Colleges and Business Partnerships ................ 17 *by William J. Hierstein* | |
| Chapter 4 | Educational Reform: It's the Economy, Stupid, or Is It? ........................................................... 21 *by Stephen J. Kriedelbaugh* | |
| Chapter 5 | Advocacy for Literacy: A Blueprint for Action ........ 35 *by Ruth Mercedes Smith, Sandra Feaver, and Vicki Anderson* | |
| Chapter 6 | Minority Recruitment at Rural Colleges ................... 43 *by Julius R. Brown* | |
| Chapter 7 | External Fund Development: The Gold Medal ........ 51 *by Paul Alcantra* | |
| Chapter 8 | Evidencing Effectiveness ........................................... 57 *by W.A. Griffin, Jr.* | |

# AACC Commission on Small and/or Rural Community Colleges

July 1, 1993 - June 30, 1994

William A. Griffin, Chair
President
Mid-Plains Community College
McDonald-Belton Campus
North Platte, NE

Paul Alcantra
President
Porterville College
Kern Community College
Porterville, CA

Julius Brown
President
Wallace Community College
Selma, AL

Deborah Lee Floyd
President
Prestonsburg Community College
Prestonsburg, KY

William J. Hierstein
President
Central Maine Technical College
Auburn, ME

Stephen J. Kridelbaugh
President
Southwestern Oregon Community
 College
Coos Bay, OR

Steven W. Jones (Board Liaison)
President
Phillips County Community
 College
Helena, AR

David Hildebrand
President
Wisconsin Indianhead VTAE
 District
Shell Lake, WI

Martha A. Smith
President
Dundalk Community College
Dundalk, MD

Vicki R. Smith
President
Austin Community College
Austin, MN

Jacqueline D. Taylor
President
Fulton-Montgomery Community
   College Distrcit
Johnston, NY

James Tangeman
President
Garden City Community College
Garden City, KS

Lynn Barnett (AACC Liaison)
Director of Community
   Developemt
American Association of
   Community Colleges

Belle S. Wheelan
President
Central Virginia Community
   College
Lynchburg, VA

Ruth Mercedes Smith
President
Highland Community College
Freeport, IL

# INTRODUCTION

In the fall of 1993 the Commission on Small and/or Rural Community Colleges decided to publish a monograph as the major project for the 1993-1994 commission. I agreed to serve as editor of the monograph and try to keep the project moving forward. It has been filled with challenges, but it has been a labor of love. I believe that small and rural community colleges are making a contribution to the nation that few seem to understand. More than 700 of AACC's member institutions are considered small and/or rural, and it is not easy to represent them fairly with a twelve-person commission.

The commission members were given the opportunity to write a chapter for this monograph, and what follows is the result. Jacqueline Taylor gives a good model on how our institutions can be involved in building leaders through community services. Ford Craig and W.A. Griffin, Jr., explain the role of institutional research in decision making at a small rural college. William J. Hierstein gives practical advice about getting involved with business and forming a partnership that works for both the college and business.

Perhaps the most original article is provided by Stephen J. Kridelbaugh concerning educational reform—must reading for all community college leaders. Ruth Mercedes Smith, Sandra Feaver, and Vicki Anderson give a blueprint for action in advocating literacy on our campuses. Julius R. Brown reminds us of our responsibility to recruit minorities and provides the means to accomplish this task. Paul Alcantra indicates that it is time for our institutions to get involved in external fund development. Finally, I discuss the importance of each college developing niches through examination of the mission statement, strategic planning, and assessment to evidence effectiveness.

The editor wishes to express appreciation to the AACC staff for their assistance in this project, especially Lynn Barnett. A big thanks to the staff at Mid-Plains Community College, Debra Griffin for proofing the text, and Genevieve Sharp for inputting the text.

*W.A. Griffin, Jr., Chair*
*AACC Commission on Small and/or Rural Community Colleges*
*April 1994*

# CHAPTER ONE

# BUILDING LEADERS THROUGH COMMUNITY SERVICE

### *Jacqueline D. Taylor*

"Be ashamed to die until you have won some victory for humanity" was the motto of Horace Mann, the founding president of Antioch College. This entrepreneurial leader's call to community service is echoed by Kouzes and Posner (1988) with their claim that when one gives back some of what one has been given, one can reconstruct communities and renew the foundations of democracy. Thomas Cronin believes that community service opportunities help build leaders "who can help create options . . . who can help clarify problems and choices, who can build morale and coalitions, who can inspire others and provide a vision of the possibilities and promise of a better organization, or a better community" (Rosenbach and Taylor, 1993, p. 12).

We should pause for a moment and consider the significance of the service mission for building our future leaders. Combining the energies of our college students with seasoned leaders who care and have committed themselves to a lifetime of service can revitalize our communities and value systems. The vitality of America lies in our ability to educate and nourish more citizen leaders.

On September 21, 1993, President Clinton signed into law the National and Community Service Trust Act, which amended the previous National and Community Service Trust Act of 1990. The legislation created the Corporation for National Service, which oversees AmeriCorps, an initiative that distributes awards to help finance students' college education or pay back student loans in return for one or two years of service.

AmeriCorps' chief executive officer, Eli Segal, states that "national service is one of the tools we have to fix our communities, (although) not the only tool. Its ultimate moral purpose is getting things done in the community. There are other worthwhile by-products. We certainly believe the citizen ethic it fosters is legitimate. We think at a time when there are so many centrifugal forces which pull us apart, service is a vehicle to pull communities together" (Zook, 1993).

This effort to pull communities together will be reinforced by the AmeriCorps plan to give large numbers of students minimum wage, education credit, and a $4,725 living stipend for each year of service performed, up to two years. The focus remains on the necessity for learning and rebuilding communities through community service and not on the wages and education credit. However, this service credit does emphasize the significant role that can be addressed when educational institutions and communities join together for the betterment of society, and it is a key component. Jim Mahoney states, "In three years the Office of National Service believes 100,000 full-time volunteers will be in place" (1993, p. 9). This is a tremendous investment in people and dollars: the federal government has committed to rebuilding communities and developing future leaders by combining education and service. Robert Atwell, president of the American Council on Education, emphasized the significance of this program when he said it would lead to a "renaissance of community spirit" (Mahoney, 1993, p. 9).

What organization is more closely linked with the community and more able to engender a collective renaissance than the community college? The size of a college makes no significant difference, nor whether it is rural, suburban, or urban, single- or multicampus. The need to connect with and serve the community transcends all boundaries. The focus is on rebuilding the spirit and value of community service and improving the community through caring.

## CARING: A MAJOR COMPONENT OF LEADERSHIP

"Genuine caring is an integral attribute of effective leadership, and may, in fact, be the most important component," according to John D. Barkham, a Michigan community leader, mentor, and business entrepreneur who has devoted his life to community service, particularly at Michigan State University. Barkham believes that taking the time, energy, and enthusiasm to care and give of one's self to improve the community can diminish dependence upon "government doing" and focus on the responsibility of the individual citizen to give something back to one's community. In his estimation, "Individuals taking action based upon caring as the underlying motivator serve to help reestablish values and community." In support of this description of a caring leader, Cronin quotes Michael Maccoby: "A developed heart implies integrity, a spiritual center, a sense of 'I' not motivated by greed or fear, but by love of life, adventure and fellow feelings" (1993, p. 22). Maccoby feels that a leader cannot allow a shell to build up around his or her heart, and so he emphasizes the caring aspect of leadership. Cronin states that "people can achieve meaning in their lives only when they can give as well as take from a society" (p. 17).

Jay L. Robinson writes that John Dewey, an avid proponent of joining theory and practice, declared, "All members of a democratic society were entitled to an education that would enable them to make the best of themselves as active participants in the life of their community; . . . To extend the range and the fullness of sharing in the intellectual and spiritual resources of community is the very meaning of the community." Dewey further argued that, to be an effective member of a democracy, a person must have "training in science, in art, in history, command of the fundamental methods of inquiry, and the fundamental tools of intercourse and communication," as well as "a trained eye and hand; habits of industry, perseverance, and above all, habits of serviceableness" (p. 9).

This "serviceableness," as Dewey called service to community or humanity, is a lifelong commitment for community college students, who are themselves lifelong learners and closely linked to their local communities through families, jobs, and education. Phi Theta Kappa, the community college honor society, is in essence a "service society that calls for its members to "serve your community, through projects targeted to specific problem areas, and by your participation in fund drives that turn over a portion of their proceeds to local organizations" (Phi Theta Kappa Leadership Manual, p. 27).

The Phi Theta Kappa focus on excellence in academics and

leadership combined with commitment to service prepares students with the desire and discipline to fully participate in life, for, as John Kennedy reminded Americans, "The educated citizen has an obligation to serve the public . . . [as] a participant and not as a spectator." Cronin echoes this obligation to serve when he states that "America generally prizes participation in all kinds of organizations, especially civic and political" (p. 13).

This blend of commitment to life and service, undergirded with a strong fabric of academic excellence, helps students develop leadership skills. Rosenbach and Taylor declare that "if, as we believe, leadership is based upon confidence, self-knowledge, and introspection, then a thorough grounding in history, literature, the arts, language, and human behavior is appropriate training for leadership" (p. 2).

## NATIONAL COMPACTS FOR COMMUNITY SERVICE

While community colleges are linked closely to the community through missions to address local needs, all colleges and universities can combine human and financial resources to provide community service pathways. Joint ventures between colleges and universities and K-12 school districts benefit students and the communities they serve. An example is the National Campus Compact, with member colleges and universities in states such as California, Michigan, and Pennsylvania. This organization is already on the cutting edge of community service and is prepared to assist AmeriCorps as it implements the National Service Act. Unique partnerships have been formed among undergraduate and graduate, two-year and four-year, and public and private institutions. In Michigan such service-oriented organizations as the Kellogg and Kresge foundations joined in launching the state compact.

A portion of the compact's mission statement refers to promoting education for citizenship by encouraging service and internship experiences that develop students' sense of civic responsibility. According to the statement, "Real-world experiences introduce students to civic involvement and lay the foundation for a lifelong ethic of public responsibility and community service that will enable them to become committed, compassionate citizens" (Michigan Campus Compact, 1993). Cronin sees compassion and caring as important components of community service: he advocates that "leaders exhibit an emotion, a passion for what they are doing."

The compact's mission statement also says, "Community service that addresses society's urgent needs can do more than any single course alone to make social responsibility a central part of student life." This focus on creating lifelong commitment to service blends "unlimited talents with finite resources" and provides opportunities for leadership development and training through giving of one's self, seeing what needs to be done, and developing ways to make a difference (Michigan Campus Compact, 1993). "To a leader making a difference is important" (Rosenbach and Taylor, 1993, p. 3). The compact holds annual leadership camps and student conferences with the goal of building leadership skills with a service emphasis. The compact is trying to stop the erosion of values that has become a major problem in U.S. society.

The methods of connecting the classroom to the community are many. One excellent method, service learning credit, gives students credit for service projects as a segment of the course assignment or for service internships in community agencies. Holding a community service and volunteer agency fair on campus familiarizes students, faculty, administrators, and staff with the community's problems and needs. It also gives attendees a chance to determine how their talents and interests match community needs. This exposure can be a first link between the student as volunteer and the community.

## SERVICE LEARNING RESOURCES

The University of Michigan's Office of Community Service Learning, through a grant from the Michigan Campus Compact, has published *Praxis I: A Faculty Casebook on Community Service Learning* (Golura, et al., 1993a) and *Praxis II: Service-Learning Resources for University Students, Staff and Faculty* (Golura, et al., 1993b). These resources are excellent for faculty interested in adding a service learning dimension to their classrooms. Each community college, four-year college, or university has its own connections with the community, and each has unlimited human resources in students who are motivated and talented and who want to help improve this nation. Connecting the energy, enthusiasm, and caring attitude of a multitude of students with problems to be solved provides a learning pathway that addresses societal concerns and builds leaders.

Organizations such as Habitat for Humanity have encouraged students in construction technology classes to participate in building and remodeling homes as service learning and practical application projects. At Fulton-Montgomery Community College, New York, students in the Human Services and Early Childhood Education programs volunteer to work in community agencies and receive academic credit for it. Into the Streets, an annual community cleanup project in many cities, focuses the energies and enthusiasm of thousands of students for community betterment. These are but a few of the possibilities when students and community agencies join to attack the challenges that face communities throughout the nation.

## REFLECTIONS

When students take the initiative to give back to the community, they develop skills that are applicable throughout a lifetime. The Michigan Campus Compact has identified several skills gained through service learning: leadership, listening, problem-solving, team-building, collaboration, and self-discipline. Stephen C. Halpern points out that "in doing work with the community, we must listen to the voices within the community" (1992, p. 44). This ability to listen was also identified by the Michigan Campus Compact as a skill gained through community service. Halpern also writes, "The real question is not whether we are linked to the larger society, but how we are linked to it and whose interests we advance and serve through that linkage" (p. 46). His theory is that "part of being a liberally educated person is understanding the value and ethic of serving others—of using one's talents and energies on behalf of others, without expecting or getting any material benefit in return" (p. 47). He states that it is invaluable for students to learn the enormous satisfaction that can come from serving others. It is critical for educators to nurture that understanding. He also confirms the need for presidential commitment and support if a community service program is to be successful.

Arlene Sitterly, a long-time community leader in upstate New York who was also an early role model for businesswomen, complimented Fulton-Montgomery Community College, New York, on its community involvement, but her comments could apply to any community college. She said, "The college faculty, staff and administrators are role models for students, and their community involvement establishes a pattern of positive influence for the student body. It also creates the opportunity for students and faculty to cooperate for the betterment of the community, and makes a strong statement of the importance and value of volunteerism as a community linkage." This reinforces Halpern's theory that "when colleges and universities value serving others and encourage students to engage in service, and when students see their professors doing that, that sends an important message that can counterbalance the neurotic and destructive self-centeredness that dominates our culture" (p. 47).

It is the responsibility of individuals to return to society some of what they have been given, to participate, to share their talents with others in community service. It is also the responsibility of colleges and universities to encourage this higher order of commitment and caring, and provide community service links and opportunities. In doing so, we not only help solve community problems, we build future leaders who care about others. The skills of community service and leadership transcend all boundaries, geographic or economic; these are skills that can take the individual through a lifetime of giving and caring, of envisioning, accomplishing, motivating and inspiring, and above all, of believing in and valuing the opportunity to serve humanity.

To advocate building leaders through community service, one must believe in John Gardner's four moral goals of leadership. These are releasing human potential, balancing the needs of the individual and the community, defending the fundamental values of the community, and instilling in individuals a sense of initiative and responsibility. Kouzes and Posner say attending to these goals will always lift an individual's eyes to higher purposes. As each of us serves the values of freedom, justice, equality, caring, and dignity, the foundations of democracy are constantly renewed, and as each of us takes responsibility for creating the world of our dreams, we can all participate in leading. Tying leadership to community service is the true essence of Atwell's "renaissance of community spirit," which is so important to revitalizing our nation's value system.

*Jacqueline D. Taylor is president of Fulton-Montgomery Community College, New York.*

## REFERENCES

Bennis, Warren. *An Invented Life: Reflections on Leadership and Change.* Reading, Mass.: Addison-Wesley, 1993.

Cronin, Thomas. "Reflections on Leadership." In Rosenbach, William E., and Taylor, Robert L. (Eds). *Contemporary Issues in Leadership.* Boulder, Colo.: Westview Press, 1993, pp. 7–25.

Golura, Joseph, et al. *Praxis I: A Faculty Casebook on Community Service Learning.* Ann Arbor, Mich.: Office of Community Service Learning Press, 1993a.

Golura, Joseph, et al. *Praxis II: Service-Learning Resources for University Students, Staff and Faculty.* Ann Arbor, Mich.: Office of Community Service Learning Press, 1993b.

Halpern, Stephen C. "University-Community Projects: Reflections on the Lessons Learned." *Universities and Community Schools.* Fall-Winter 1992, *3* (1–2), 44–48.

Kouzes, James M. and Posner, Barry Z. *The Leadership Challenge: How to Get Extraordinary Things Done in Organizations.* San Francisco: Jossey-Bass, 1988.

Mahoney, James. "Launching National Service." *Community College Times.* November 30, 1993, p. 9.

Michigan Campus Compact. *Michigan Campus Compact: An Overview.* East Lansing, Mich.: Michigan Campus Compact, 1993.

Morton, Keith. "Models of Service and Civic Education." Occasional paper of the project on integrating service and academic study. East Lansing, Mich.: Michigan Campus Compact, 1993.

Phi Theta Kappa. *Phi Theta Kappa Leadership Manual.*

Robinson, Jay L. "An Editorial Statement." *On Common Ground.* Fall 1993, pp. 4–5, 8–9.

Rosenbach, William E., and Taylor, Robert L. (Eds). *Contemporary Issues in Leadership.* Boulder, Colo.: Westview Press, 1993.

Vivian, Executive Editor. "On Common Ground." Yale-New Haven Teachers Institute. Fall 1993, (1), 9.

Zook, Jim. "National Service Races to Get into Gear." *Chronicle of Higher Education,* December 8, 1993, p. A32.

## CHAPTER TWO

# THE ROLE OF INSTITUTIONAL RESEARCH AT A SMALL RURAL COMMUNITY COLLEGE

*Ford Craig and W.A. Griffin, Jr.*

While most colleges struggle with limited finances and human resources, small and rural community colleges are especially affected by these limitations. Because of these constraints, small and rural community colleges must manage their limited resources more wisely than ever before. Decision-makers cannot make decisions off the cuff. What is needed is the type of information that is essential to effective decision making: the kind of information available from institutional research. "The success or failure of any community college today depends primarily on the ability of its top-level leadership to make valid, efficient, and effective decisions, decisions based on pertinent and reliable research data" (Zeiss, 1986, p. 35). An effective institutional research office assists administrators, faculty, and boards by providing information on the college's operations, product, and target market. How do students feel about the quality of the college's instruction, student services, and recreational opportunities? What new programs are needed, and must any be eliminated? A maintained database on basic services, coupled with valid survey data, can assist decision-makers in these and a host of other areas. Institutional research data will not necessarily ensure that all decisions will be the right ones. However, reviewing information provided by the institutional research office will help leaders make more informed, and therefore better, decisions.

What kinds of information do institutional researchers provide? In a 1989 survey, practicing institutional research officers ranked three dozen frequent tasks (Volkwein, 1990). The tasks ranged from enrollment reporting to space-allocation statistics and analysis. Enrollment management studies topped the list. Other frequent tasks included conducting studies on attrition; reporting enrollment data, student characteristics, and national survey data; analyzing faculty workload; and surveying student opinion.

## MPCCA Experience

The experiences of Mid-Plains Community College Area (MPCCA), Nebraska, a small, rural, multicampus institution, serve as an example of how important the work of the office of institutional research can be. These experiences are typical of those at similar schools. The function of institutional research is relatively new to MPCCA. As a result of a recent North Central Association accreditation study, the need for uniform and unified data became obvious. Certain kinds of data, such as student headcount numbers, could be found in abundance, albeit with minor discrepancies. However, data on how well MPCCA graduates performed after leaving the college were sketchy and anecdotal at best. It was out of this experience that the MPCCA institutional research function was created.

After these data problems associated with the self-study process became apparent, one of the authors, Ford Craig, conducted research on how to best organize the MPCCA institutional research function. Craig completed a doctoral paper that included a literature review and a survey of thirty administrators in the MPCCA system (a 96.7 percent response rate). Based on his findings, several recommendations were made, including:

- that the MPCCA Governing Board create and fund a director of institutional research position
- that the institutional research position be centralized in the district office
- that each campus location have a designated contact person through whom data would be distributed.

In addition, survey responses provided a research agenda, which consisted of needs assessment, public relations and marketing, effectiveness/outcomes studies, research to secure federal grants, studies of institutional climate, and a centralized response to independent and doctoral surveys (Craig, 1991).

The study provided valuable insight for the creation and development of the research function. The MPCCA board directed research operations to begin two days a week by late October 1991. By September 1992, the research was operating three days a week. The institutional research director staffs a one-person office part-time and continues teaching on a reduced schedule. The MPCCA staffing pattern is somewhat typical of many small or rural community colleges: "They are one-person offices, unlikely to grow over time into ten person (or more) units or decentralized networks of analysts that exist in a few large and complex institutions" (Presley, 1990, p. 2).

A partial listing of the director's typical activities follows:

*Regional Accreditation Support Data.* These are collected each year and organized through descriptive statistics, tables, and graphs. Short memos are distributed to target audiences including governing board members, administrators, faculty, and staff (when appropriate).

*Follow-up data on graduates.* These are collected from receiving institutions (when available) and from locally generated and administered follow-up surveys. Again, research memos incorporating findings of follow-up studies are subsequently written and distributed to appropriate audiences.

*Student Assessment Activities.* These are facilitated by the director, who chairs a task force on assessment. Members of this group guide the development of a districtwide assessment plan intended to document MPCCA student academic achievement. Measures integral to the plan include an entering student placement test and a system of student surveys. Data secured through assessment activities is analyzed, organized, and disseminated by the institutional research office.

*MPCCA Strategic Planning Data.* These are collected, analyzed, and made available to key audiences. Such data include past and present enrollment trends, MPCCA general population demographics, and area high school enrollment and economic trends.

*Staff/Faculty Surveys.* The director, in coordination with other administrators, conducted a faculty and staff organizational functioning survey and a faculty and administrator survey. Both address institutional climate and degree of satisfaction. As with the aforementioned student survey, summary reports of results were written and distributed to the governing board, administration, faculty, and staff.

*Student-Right-to-Know Data.* These crime statistics and persistence/completion data are collected, analyzed, and reported. This task is complicated somewhat by the lack of a centralized computing system for student records. Data are collected from each campus location and merged into system data.

*External Data Requests.* The director also responds to or coordinates (in cooperation with other key administrators) a wide variety of surveys and data requests to external groups and agencies. Requesting agencies have included: Morgan Community College, Iowa Central Community College, Barton County Community College, Nebraska Community College Association, the American Association of Community Colleges, the *Chronicle of Higher Education,* the National Center for Educational Statistics, the Higher Education Research Institute Survey, the Nebraska Postsecondary Coordinating Commission, First Presbyterian Church of North Platte, Educom, the PEQIS Survey System, the North Central Association, the Oklahoma Board of Regents for Higher Education, a local McCook newspaper, the *Peterson's Guide,* and the Noel Levitz Center for Enrollment Management.

*Library.* A small collection of books is maintained and shelved in the Institutional Research Office. Series maintained include *New Directions in Institutional Research, Research in Higher Education,* and *New Directions in Community Colleges.* Recent publications concerning institutional research, assessment, and planning issues in community colleges form part of the mini-administrative library. A list of these resources is published periodically and MPCCA administrators have intermittently used them.

These represent a number of the institutional research tasks performed in this small, rural community college system. It is a job that is necessary, energizing, and frustrating—sometimes all of these in one day. However, the rewards and payoffs are there, if one can derive satisfaction from watching people use the office of institutional research to make the institution a better place to be for all.

*Ford Craig is the institutional research director of Mid-Plains Community College, Nebraska. W.A. Griffin, Jr. is president of the McDonald-Belton Campus of Mid-Plains Community College.*

## REFERENCES

Clagett, Craig A. and Huntington, Robin B. *The Institutional Research Practitioner: A Guidebook to Effective Performance.* Silver Spring, Md.: Red Inc. Publications, 1990.

Craig, Ford M. "An Assessment of How to Organize Effectively the Function of Institutional Research in the Mid-Plains Technical Community College Area." Unpublished report. Fort Lauderdale, Fla.: NOVA University, 1991.

Presley, Jennifer B. *Organizing effective institutional research offices.* New Directions for Institutional Research, No. 66. San Francisco: Jossey-Bass. Summer 1990.

Volkwein, J. Fredericks. "The Diversity of Institutional Research Structures and Tasks." In J.B. Presley (Ed.), *Organizing effective institutional research offices.* New Directions in Institutional Research, No. 66. San Francisco: Jossey-Bass. Summer 1990.

Zeiss, P. Anthony. "Strategic Management via Institutional Research." In J. Losak (Ed.), *Applying Institutional Research in Decision Making.* New Directions for Community Colleges, No. 56. San Francisco: Jossey-Bass, Winter 1986.

# CHAPTER THREE

# SMALL COLLEGES AND BUSINESS PARTNERSHIPS

### *William J. Hierstein*

Small colleges often have difficulty imagining themselves in partnerships with business. They work hard to provide educational services to business upon request, but partnerships often seem out of reach. The concept of partnership goes beyond the occasional service that all community and technical colleges try to provide to local business and its employees. Partnerships involve continuing, mutually advantageous relationships through which both parties profit. They usually are formalized by contract but can be done on a handshake when appropriate.

Small colleges in rural or small-town settings often envy larger, more urban institutions that seem to have the resources, personnel, and contacts necessary to attract such partnerships and reap their benefits. They imagine having a center for business and industry, instead of one or two people in the continuing education division scurrying around promoting services for business and industry. In fact, even identifying businesses for potential partnership relationships is often difficult away from the cities. Often there is one large manufacturing operation nearby with its own training department, and although it is generous to the foundation, donates surplus equipment, and employs graduates on those rare occasions when it is hiring, there doesn't seem to be much opportunity for meaningful partnership.

There may be a few small manufacturing plants, usually subsidiaries of larger companies with headquarters in other places. Again, though the college occasionally can provide continuing and adult education classes to their employees, partnership opportunities are limited because the real decision-making power lies with the parent companies.

The remaining businesses in the small-college service area tend to be small retail and service operations, many locally owned. There are some franchises and a few retail or service outlets, but they are usually small with relatively few employees—hardly fertile ground for partnerships. So a small college often waits and dreams of the "new plant," always just over the horizon, that will come to town because the college can provide a highly trained workforce—every president's dream of an economic development coup.

But small colleges have some advantages when developing business partnerships. Most notably, small colleges can eliminate the layers of bureaucracy needed to reach agreement. There are also more direct lines of control to ensure successful implementation. There is an attention to quality that is sometimes lost with a larger scale.

A rural setting, too, can be turned to an advantage. One can still get a hotel room for less than fifty dollars in a small community. Companies bringing employees into a major city for training would be lucky to pay twice that. It may be faster, even safer, to drive from a major airport to a suburban or rural community than to drive into the city center.

There is certainly less overhead at a smaller college. Lab or shop space can usually be rented and instructional costs usually are more reasonable. The low cost of doing business in a rural area can be a powerful lure.

A college seeking to establish partnerships should examine not only its needs but its strengths. Quality sells. For the small college, quality usually is vested in technical programs or transfer offerings that have outstanding faculty. It is easy to sell star performers. Developing partnerships that build on areas of strength often allows colleges to improve in areas of need as funds replaced through the partnership are recommitted.

The first rule for a college trying to find business partnerships is: Don't be afraid to ask. If you never ask, they will never say no, but they will also never have the opportunity to say yes. The second is: Use your contacts. A local representative, an advisory council member for instance, can lead you to the parent company. Even a good customer can help. The third rule is: Get what you want and don't promise more than you can deliver; and the fourth rule is: Pay attention after the sale. Partnerships often start small and need to be developed. Remember that they are mutually advantageous. Don't try to take all the marbles and run.

It also is important to realize that small businesses not only can lead you to big business partners but often are in a position to form small partnerships. Sometimes a consortium of small related businesses can band together to accomplish a large partnership goal. Some examples of partnerships implemented at Central Maine Technical College are:

- A joint venture radiography program with the largest of the area's hospitals. The hospital supplies the lab and instructors, and the college supplies core instruction and has degree-granting authority.
- An occupational health and safety associate degree program funded primarily by contributions from three large industries. This partnership was formed when state funding was not available for the project. Maine has the highest per capita rate of worker injuries in the country. Industry recognized the need, the college was responsive, and industry has paid the bill through 1995.
- An agreement with a licensed distributor for SmartCAM software provides for free updates in return for limited use of college lab and machine tool equipment in demonstrating its software.
- An agreement with a consortium of twenty-six hospitals, nursing homes, and home health care providers that enables the college to expand its nursing program into the community. Instructors' salaries, clinical facilities, and scholarship support for students are provided by the consortium. The consortium hopes to reduce the shortage of registered nurses in the area.
- A formal partnership arrangement with Ford Motor Company that established a Ford-specific automotive training program, the ASSET program, at Central Maine Technical College. The college provides in-service training for Ford technicians in Maine.
- An arrangement that provides technical assistance and training to employees of a local television station in return for production of video presentations about the college.
- A robotics lab furnished in large part by a local industry with which the college has a long-standing relationship. The industry is now

moving toward a more flexible manufacturing format and has a developing need for robotics technicians. Robotics instruction is the next logical step in the development of the college's electromechanical technology program.

These examples demonstrate the give-and-take nature of good partnerships and the value of such arrangements to a small college. Good partnerships can bring resources and students to the college. They can be a shot in the arm for faculty and staff. They can bring good publicity and higher visibility in the local community.

Small colleges can form successful business and industry partnerships. They need to recognize their strengths and aggressively seek partners. It is not easy, but it is not impossible. For a small college, the payoff in resources make them worth the effort.

*William J. Hierstein is president of Central Maine Technical College.*

## REFERENCES

Cetron, M.J. "School-Business Partnership." *The Futurist,* November/December 1988, *22,* 12.

Currin, E.C., Jr. "The Community College's Role in Rural Economic Development." *Community/Junior College Quarterly of Research and Practice,* 1988, *12* (1), 37–46.

Epstein, J.L. "Paths to Partnership: What We Can Learn From Federal, State, District, and School Initiatives." *Phi Delta Kappa,* January 1991, *72* (5), 344–349.

Gianini, P.C. "Islands of Innovation: New and Small Community Services in the Small/Rural Community College." Paper presented at the Annual Convention of the American Association of Community Colleges, April 29–May 2, 1979. (ED 170 004)

Glennon, M. "Fund Raising in Small Colleges: Strategies for Success." *Planning for Higher Education,* 1985-86, *14* (3), 16–29.

Peck, R.D. "The Entrepreneurial College Presidency." *Educational Record,* Winter 1983, *64* (1), 18–25.

# CHAPTER FOUR

# EDUCATIONAL REFORM: IT'S THE ECONOMY, STUPID, OR IS IT?

*Stephen J. Kridelbaugh*

Although reform has always been a part of the history of education, educational reform as we know it today began in 1982 with the publication of *A Nation at Risk,* which described the dramatic decline in students' academic performance in the K-12 educational system since the end of the Second World War. The study outlined a direct negative correlation between the relatively poor academic performance of American youth in the basics of reading, writing, and mathematics and America's economic competitiveness. If our workers were not competent, we would not be able to compete in the world economy, and the American middle class would decline.

The report also pointed out that not all segments of our society were participating in or benefiting from education proportionally. Because women, minorities, and immigrants were going to be the principal source of new labor over the next ten to fifteen years, their participation and success rates at all educational levels had to be raised, or the nation's vitality would be jeopardized. Elements of these problems have been discussed extensively over the past decade.

## ECONOMIC COMPETITIVENESS

How can the nation compete when its citizenry is poorly educated and ill prepared for work? Business leaders not only complained of insufficient academic preparation, but that America's young adults had an extremely poor work ethic. Over the past decade, thousands of articles, books, talk shows, workshops, and symposia highlighted the problem.

American students were no longer the best prepared in the world. Functional illiteracy approached a frightening level: 40 to 60 percent of the adult population, depending on the information source. The K-12 system bears a large responsibility for the decline in economic competitiveness.

Although the vast majority of criticisms and prescriptions were directed at the K-12 system, community colleges and four-year institutions became swept up in the discussion. For higher education the attacks were mainly limited to access, costs, and quality of instruction, especially in students' first two years.

As the national discussion on reform continued into the late eighties, it was found that significant segments of American society were not participating fully in our educational systems, especially African Americans, Hispanics, and native Americans. Although women now constitute a majority in higher education, they are still underrepresented in the physical sciences and mathematics. The graduation rates for minorities from high school and college did not reflect their proportions in the general population. If the nation is to succeed in its quest to remain an economic world power, minorities and women need to be more fully integrated into, and succeed in, all segments of our educational systems. Between 70 and 80 percent of the increase in our workforce by 2000 will come from these population segments and immigrants.

Another factor in the equation of educational reform was added to the formula for success in the late eighties through such works as *The Neglected Majority,* and *The Forgotten Half: Non College Youth in America.* Both described in detail the fact that 50 percent of the high school population was not going on to college. Many of these people were not even graduating from high school. Estimates of a 50 percent dropout rate in inner cities and a national rate exceeding 20 percent substantiated these claims.

In the past, especially during the fifties, sixties, and seventies, dropouts could enter the world of employment with excellent wages and benefits. During that epoch we were the economic powerhouse of the developed world. However, in the mid-seventies this began to change, and by the end of the eighties a high school diploma did not guarantee a job that would maintain a person, let alone a family, at a middle class level. In fact, beginning in the eighties many college graduates were unable to obtain jobs and salary levels that their educational sacrifices would have guaranteed in the past. The middle class was becoming harder to attain, especially for the untrained. These people worked dead-end service industry jobs that paid poorly and did not provide adequate health care or other benefits. Many studies indicated that a majority of jobs in the new workplace would require education beyond high school, but not a bachelor's degree.

## PROFESSIONAL/TECHNICAL TRAINING

It became clear that our educational system was going to have to produce far more students trained in vocational disciplines. It has been axiomatic in this country that continuing one's education meant studying for a bachelor's degree. Our society has looked down its nose at those employed in vocational fields, except when we have to write a check for their services.

Among other national education systems, Germany's became the favorite model because of the overall performance of its students and the dual nature of its secondary educational system in respect to vocational and college preparatory programs. German sixteen-year-olds are tracked into a professional/technical or college preparatory program based on examinations and personal interests. The German model provided more than enough well-trained employees in professional/technical areas. Germany also has a mature national manpower planning program, and German business, industry, and labor are active participants in professional/technical training in secondary schools, apprenticeships, and the workplace. Professional/technical training in Germany continues through the first two years of college, followed by lifelong learning.

Many refer to the changes in our educational system as the "new vocationalism." There is nothing new about it. I graduated from Wilbur Wright High School in Detroit, Michigan, in 1956. Wright High was a trade school where I majored in tool and die manufacturing. In my junior and senior years, I alternated between working for two weeks at Maks

Machine Company, a tool and die shop, and attending school for two weeks. Upon graduation, I entered the apprenticeship program for tool and die makers. At Wright students had the option of taking vocational or college preparatory courses such as physics, advanced algebra, and chemistry. All of the vocational programs at Wright contained the major elements of the "new vocationalism" and current proposals for educational reform: school-to-work transition, on-the-job training, employer involvement, career planning, job-related training in the last two years of high school followed by further technical training, extensive involvement between education and business, and the option to take courses leading to college admission. Decisions about occupation were made at the age of sixteen. Wilbur Wright High School is now called Murray Wright High School and is no longer a trade school. What happened to these types of high schools and vocational programs? No one needed them when students could go to a major company and earn $15 an hour with excellent benefits.

Educational reform has to make professional/technical careers more attractive for youth, their counselors, and parents. Business has to take a more proactive and responsible role in working with education and providing work experience and training for professional/technical students. We have done it before, and we can do it again.

## Accountability

Throughout the eighties, accountability was always a significant element of any discussion relating to our educational system's failure to prepare our citizenry for the new economic world order. Initially it alone was blamed for the nation's predicament. Only in the last two to three years have disintegration of the family, vast changes in values and morals, individual responsibility, and business responsibility become topics in the popular debate about the performance of American youth, their educational success, and the nation's economic competitiveness.

As the economy changed from a manufacturing base to a service base, it became apparent that each worker's success depended on continuous upgrading of academic and personal skills to remain competitive. What started out in the eighties as a blue-collar issue, has now with downsizing engulfed hundreds of thousands of white-collar workers. Today everyone, regardless of educational preparation, has equal opportunity to become unemployed.

American business has implemented many managerial and organizational changes to compete better in the world economy; these same programs can help schools produce an educated citizenry that will help the United States to retain its economic preeminence. The publication *The Search for Excellence* in 1982 gave great impetus to the revolution in business and education. Other books and reports followed throughout the eighties, on topics such as Japanese organizational and management theory and total quality management. Business has moved on to other prescriptions such as downsizing and *Reengineering the Corporation,* as proposed by Michael Hammer and James Champy, the current gurus of change in business and industry. The educational enterprise has downsizing and reengineering to look forward to in the not-too-distant future, and we will in the process—it is hoped—become high-performance organizations.

## TODAY

The definitive work on educational reform that is going to take our educational institutions into the future was published in 1990: *America's Choice: High Skills or Low Wages.* The basic premise of *America's Choice* is that our slow economic growth is tied to the low growth rate of productivity. The solution is the high-performance work organization. This concept requires a well-educated and well-trained workforce. The problems, issues, and solutions described in *America's Choice* are driving today's educational reforms at the state and federal levels. The major recommendations found in *America's Choice* are:

*The Foundation Skills.* A new national educational performance standard should be set for all students, to be met by age sixteen. This standard would be benchmarked to the highest in the world.

*Universal Mastery of the Foundation Skills.* States should take responsibility for ensuring that virtually all students achieve a certificate of initial mastery. Through new local employment and training boards, states, with federal assistance, would create and fund alternative learning environments for those who cannot attain the certificate of initial mastery in regular schools.

*Technical and Professional Education.* A comprehensive system of technical and professional certificates and associate degrees should be created for the majority of students and adult workers who do not pursue a bachelor's degree.

*Technical Learning and High-Performance Work Organizations.* All employers should be given incentives to invest in the further education and training of their workers and to pursue high-productivity forms of work organization.

*A System to Pull it Together.* A system of employment and training boards should be established by the federal and state governments, together with local leadership, to organize and oversee new school-to-work transition programs and training systems.

A majority of the issues and their proposed solutions described in *America's Choice* are being acted on now by federal and state legislatures. Solutions found in the book form the centerpiece of President Clinton's legislative proposals for educational reform. The significant elements of *America's Choice* that have found their way into President Clinton's legislative agenda are accountability, school-to-work transition, one-stop career centers, and technical-professional training initiatives.

*Accountability.* Congress' 1992 rewrite of the U.S. Higher Education Act of 1965 creates state agencies that have, through the State Postsecondary Review Entity Program, the power to close a college down and deny federal funds to institutions with default rates greater than 25 percent in Title IV federal financial aid programs.

The U.S. Department of Education has threatened to take over all regional accreditation processes. The department proposed this during the Higher Education Act rewrite. Discussions between the department and the education associations located at the National Center for Higher

Education averted this. As a result of these talks, the regional accreditation associations will take on the accountability mandate. There are ongoing discussions involving accreditation, and the department has proposed accreditation regulations for the state postsecondary review agencies and the regional accreditation associations. The proposed questions that state postsecondary review agencies and regional accreditation associations will now ask are quite onerous: How many students are graduating? How many students are employed in their field of educational specialization? How does business rate the employee training by the institution? How do students rate their educational experience? What is the student/faculty ratio? What are the expenditures per full-time student? How do graduates' salaries compare with tuition? What are the processes to ensure that faculty are kept up to date in their specialty fields? To be sure, the regional associations will still be interested in governance models and in faculty and staff development plans, but outcome- or performance-based educational models is a concept whose time has come.

Ability-to-Benefit regulations mandate that if students without high school diplomas cannot prove academic viability by passing a skills examination, the federal government will not support their education beyond high school through Title IV.

In November 1993 two oversight hearings held on the Pell Grant program by the Senate Permanent Subcommittee on Investigations examined serious abuses of the Pell Grant program by twenty-one Orthodox Jewish schools on the East Coast. Community colleges may also be subject to this kind of oversight hearing: If religious postsecondary schools can cheat the federal government out of millions of dollars, why not public and private institutions of higher education?

With the proposed Goals 2000: Educate America Act, President Clinton will introduce legislation to establish national testing standards. The act would create a National Skills Standards Board establishing voluntary academic and work skills standards. These standards will be developed jointly by business and labor for major occupational job clusters.

*School-to-Work Transition.* Within Department of Labor appropriations is three million dollars for model community education and training centers that will assist students in school-to-work transition. Now meandering its way through Congress is President Clinton's school-to-work transition legislation, which has three components for all such programs: work-based learning, school-based learning, and connecting activities that coordinate the involvement of employers, schools students, trainers, teachers, mentors, and counselors. This extensive and important piece of legislation mandates work-based and school-based components. Each work-based plan must contain a program of job training, workplace mentoring, paid work experience, and student workplace competencies. Each school-based plan must contain career exploration/counseling, mentoring of students to help them select a career and major, and an evaluation/remediation component to ensure that students obtain required skills and knowledge. The legislation for the school-to-work programs calls for measuring and evaluating program performance and outcomes. The school-to-work transition program will be jointly administered by the Labor and Education departments.

*One-Stop Career Centers.* The Reemployment Act of 1994 provides a comprehensive worker-adjustment program and one-stop career centers. The centers will give the unemployed information about current job openings and training, testing for educational deficiencies, and career counseling. They will also provide recruitment and applicant screening for employers.

*Technical-Professional Training Initiatives.* The Scientific and Advanced-Technology Act has passed Congress and will provide funds to improve advanced technological education through the associate degree level. The act will be administered by the National Science Foundation. Initially, the foundation will fund up to five model centers for advanced technology training that will serve as information sources on curricula and on instructional methods and materials for two-year postsecondary institutions.

In 1993 Congress passed legislation to promote articulation between high schools and two-year colleges for professional/technical training programs and to develop common curricula in vocational programs, so that training will be seamless for students moving from the secondary to the postsecondary education system.

## THE OREGON EXPERIENCE

With the passage of Oregon House Bill 3565 in the spring of 1991, *America's Choice* has also defined Oregon's path to reform. House Bill 3565's enabling language states that Oregon is to have the best-educated workforce in the United States by 2000 and the best educated workforce in the world by 2010. Because of HB 3565, Oregon has become a leader in American educational reform through the following initiatives:

*Certificate of Initial and Advanced Mastery.* By age 16, all students will attain specific skill levels in critical thinking, self-directed learning oral and written communication information processing and computers, mathematics, and teamwork. A student attaining a Certificate of Initial Mastery (CIM), may opt to enter the workforce or continue to a Certificate of Advanced Mastery (CAM). The CAM program requires the student to acquire, organize, and express knowledge about a complex relationship; analyze and improve a complex process; and analyze systems, components, and interactions. The CAM will certify the knowledge and skills students need to function in their life roles and prepare them to enter employment, apprenticeships, or higher education.

There will be protection against students being shunted into educational specialties that they do not choose. Completion of CAM will allow entrance to a field of work, an apprenticeship program, or a college of choice in a vocational or academic field.

*Tech/Prep Associate Degree Programs.* To provide better training in professional/technical fields, K-12 and community college districts are to have articulated programs in six curriculum categories (or strands) through which a student in the last two years of secondary education can take courses that will directly support further training in the state's community colleges. The six strands are arts and communications, business and management, health services, human resources, industrial and engineering systems, and natural resource systems.

*Alternative Learning Centers.* For students who do not obtain either certificate by age sixteen, high school dropouts, and older adults seeking to be trained or retrained, there will be alternative learning centers ensuring that all Oregonians obtain a CIM, irrespective of learning style or age.

*Local Employment and Training Boards.* Oregon has created a state workforce quality council and sixteen regional workforce quality councils. The regional councils correspond to the geographic areas covered by Oregon's sixteen community colleges. These councils are composed of representatives from social service providers, education, and business (which is to provide the majority of members). Ultimately these councils may have the final authority in dispensing all federal training and education funds within their regions. All K-12 districts and community colleges will have to report to the councils on their student/faculty ratios, their completion/graduation rates, and the quality of education as perceived by the students and local businesses. Any grants sought from federal or state agencies relating to workforce training by educational institutions will have to be approved by the regional councils. Here accountability is aimed at providing employable graduates for the region's businesses from both K-12 schools and community colleges.

*Site Committees.* Each K-12 educational institution in Oregon will have a site committee. These are composed of faculty and classified staff and parents of children children attending. Site committees only advise the administration, but they can review and provide recommendations on any aspect of the educational program. Through site committees, the organizational/managerial concepts of the high-performance organization, such as quality circles and total quality management, will be incorporated into those facilities.

## EDUCATIONAL REFORM - WILL AT WORK

There is no doubt that the education enterprise in this country will be held accountable for its products in the future. Education will be expected to report on its successes and failures, and will be expected to rectify the failures. This may not occur as quickly or as extensively as some would like, but it will happen over time. If reform is successful, students will be better educated and more ready to enter the world of work. If a majority of its objectives are achieved at the state and national levels, American business will be better prepared to compete in the world economy. The match between the labor needs of business and the outputs of K-12 schools and community colleges will be greatly improved. At the local level we have the beginnings of a national planned manpower program. American education is expected to be a team player in meeting the training needs of youth, business, and labor. However, there are some things that the educational system cannot do. No matter how much it is said, or who says it, the American educational system cannot be held solely accountable for American economic competitiveness in the global economy.

American society will no longer tolerate a continuous growth in educational expenditures and taxation. State and federal governments are curbing costs associated with the financial grant-in-aid programs. In California, four-year graduates who wish to receive further job-related training at community colleges are now required to pay the true cost of that education, currently $50 per credit hour. Almost every state is reducing expenditures on K-12 and higher education. Even if our institutions produce the best-trained students in the world, that is not enough to guarantee that the economic diminishment of the American people will stop. International corporations will go where it is cheapest to produce goods and make a profit, and there are many variables other than quality of education in deciding where a plant will be located. As long as this country has a huge, constant foreign-trade deficit, it will not be economically healthy and cannot expect to maintain its standard of living.

On the positive side, accountability will provide a platform that will not only measure our successes, failures, strengths and weaknesses, but help to motivate everyone in our institutions to do better. We will no longer be able to hide behind tenure, perform poorly, or maintain a negative attitude.

Accountability, called "quality control" and "customer satisfaction" in business, has been the driving force for improved products and services in business over the past ten to fifteen years. The concepts that have proven successful in business will come to the public sector, including education. Through accountability we will have to manage our colleges differently and more efficiently. Mid-level managers will be eliminated, and faculty and other employees will be empowered with authority and commensurate responsibility to do their jobs, an important element of TQM.

A major concern of institutions about educational reform is that funding decisions will be made by external forces that will eliminate education programs from rural community colleges. Many rural colleges have professional/technical programs in welding, auto body repair, and machine technology, and enrollments in these programs are poor. State bureaucrats and elective officials on local employment and training boards could decide that federal funding will no longer be available to students enrolled in these programs. Such actions will ensure further enrollment decline, and ultimately the programs will be closed. The cost/benefit ratio, the bottom line in accountability, may finally win out. Such decisions will result in a serious decrease of educational opportunities for rural Americans.

Educational reform is serious, it is here now, and it will affect our institutions greatly. The federal and state governments, local employment and training boards, and accrediting associations are all going to ask questions, more often than not the same ones, about the performance of our institutions. Get prepared!

*Stephen J. Kridelbaugh is president of Southwestern Oregon Community College.*

## REFERENCES

Commission on Skills of the American Workforce. *America's Choice: High Skills or Low Wages.* Rochester, N.Y.: National Center on Education and the Economy, 1990.

Commission on Youth and America's Future. *The Forgotten Half: Non-College Youth in America.* Washington, D.C.: William T. Grant Foundation, 1988.

Hammer, Michael, and Champy, James. *Reengineering the Corporation: A Manifesto for the Business Revolution.* New York: Harper Business, 1993.

National Commission on Excellence in Education. *A Nation at Risk: The Imperative for Educational Reform.* Washington, D.C.: National

Commission on Excellence in Education, 1983.

Parnell, Dale. *The Neglected Majority.* Washington, D.C.: American Association of Community and Junior Colleges, 1985.

Peters, Thomas J., and Waterman, Robert H. *In Search of Excellence: Lessons from America's Best-Run Companies.* New York: Warner Books, 1982.

# CHAPTER FIVE

# ADVOCACY FOR LITERACY: A BLUEPRINT FOR ACTION

*Ruth Mercedes Smith, Sandra Feaver and Vicki Anderson*

"We should all be concerned about the future because we have to spend the rest of our lives there." These words by Charles Franklin Kettering remind us that we cannot escape the consequences of our actions today. This is most certainly true in the field of literacy—the small steps this nation has taken to address this critical problem have been inadequate. The consequences will affect the economic health of our nation for years to come and therefore all our lives whether or not we are literate. We read about the inadequate basic skills of our labor force, but address the problem with outdated solutions. Employers continue to state the problems: employees cannot read directions and lack analytical ability and critical thinking skills. As a result, companies cope, in the short term, by hiring experienced workers away from each other. This will not allow these companies to grow and compete in the global economy. We must expand the pool of workers who have basic workplace skills.

The future is certain to hold challenges for small and rural community colleges. Consider the following:

- Eighty percent of new jobs in the next ten years will require training beyond high school but not necessarily a four-year degree.
- By 2000, the majority of new workers will be women and minorities—many of whom have never had access to quality education.

- One in five American workers reads below an 8th-grade level.
- Three-fifths of mothers receiving welfare do not have high school diplomas.
- The average reading level of mothers on AFDC between the ages of 17 and 21 is below the 6th-grade level.
- Nearly half of female single parents have an 8th-grade education or less.
- Seventy-five percent of female heads of households without high school diplomas are living in poverty.
- Electronics will continue to affect all facets of our lives and require a higher literacy level.
- Adults will change jobs every few years and careers several times during their lifetimes, which again requires more, not fewer, basic skills and a propensity toward lifelong learning.
- In the near future it will take three workers to support each retiree. Where will they come from if one-third of the nation is undereducated?

## Tough Facts

Since the mid-eighties the need for strong literacy programs has been advocated by national and local leaders who linked poor skills with a variety of social problems range from dependence on welfare to involvement in criminal activity. We began to face up to the following disturbing facts in the 1980s:

- Between 50 and 75 percent of the unemployed are functionally illiterate.
- Of the eight million unemployed, four to six million are not trainable because of illiteracy.
- Over half of mothers on welfare support are functionally illiterate.
- Eighty-five percent of juveniles who come before the courts are functionally illiterate.
- The nation spends $6.6 billion on prison inmates, of whom 60 percent are functionally illiterate.

Jonathan Kozol was one of the first to issue the warning cry, focusing much attention on the subject of illiteracy. Kozol wrote, "The cost [of illiteracy] to our economy...is very great. The cost to our presumptions and our credibility as a democracy is greater still. The cost in needless human pain may be the greatest price of all" (1985, p. 12).

Others also rallied around the cause of literacy. The American Bar Association describes the importance of the legal profession in advocacy for literacy. "Language, especially written language, is the bedrock of civilization. The written word has enabled us to build, to learn and to remember. Through it learning and wisdom have been captured, encoded and preserved for future generations" (1987, p. 1). Forrest Chisman (1989) concludes that over twenty million adults have not mastered basic skills. Government, business, and independent research groups have created a new sense of urgency about the fate of these unfortunates. It is without a doubt one of the most serious economic problems of out time. These individuals are essential to the well-being of the nation. We cannot afford to write them off. Hunter and Harman (1979) maintain that a major shift in national education policy is needed to serve disadvantaged adults. They recommend establishing pluralistic, community-based programs to serve the most hard-core disadvantaged. The community-based initiatives would require adult students to help design programs based on concrete learning needs growing out of issues affecting their lives. Programs would involve learning by doing and would be implemented at times and places determined by their communities. We thus invest not only in these individuals, but the future of our communities and nation.

For years we have been involved in literacy efforts on local, state, and national levels. We have read reports that show no decrease in the more than 20 percent of our citizens who lack the basic literacy skills to survive economically. Neither the states nor the federal government have been willing to spend enough to eradicate the problem. We also have watched state and local organizations fight over limited funds rather than focus on finding the best ways to reach students. Public schools, literacy councils, and community and technical colleges in many states are set up to battle each other rather than be rewarded for finding solutions. In 1993 a study funded by the National Center for Education Statistics declared that the problem is even more desperate than formerly believed. The

National Adult Literacy Survey asked more than 26,000 people over the age of sixteen about their abilities to perform required functions of life. Interviewees were not asked if they could read. They were asked in approximately hour-long interviews to demonstrate their skills in prose, document, and quantitative literacy. When the results of this study are extrapolated to the U.S. population, the results are staggering. Forty-six to 51 percent of the 191 million adults in this country—88 million to 97 million people—fall into the first two levels of proficiency. According to *Time* magazine, Levels 1 and 2 are considered to be below the proficiency needed to perform a modestly demanding job.

Not all the news is bad. There have been some positive actions: Studies have been conducted, results have been tabulated, scenarios have been hypothesized, books have been written, and legislation has been debated. But what has changed? What have been the results? There have been some positive actions. When first lady Barbara Bush, made literacy her cause, several endowments, including the Barbara Bush Foundation and the Kenan Trust, began to funnel dollars into literacy-related projects and programming. The National Literacy Act was passed, creating literacy and life skills training programs for prisoners and establishing literacy programs for public housing residents. A new division of the U.S. Department of Education was created for adult education and literacy. Celebrities of all types spoke out about illiteracy and a few came forward to describe their personal struggles. Adult educators are buoyed by the knowledge that they are doing something that matters a great deal to their communities. Volunteers flock to support literacy programs with their well-meaning efforts. Community agencies are more aware of literacy issues and incorporate education more readily into their case-planning processes. More grants are available for literacy and adult education. Businesses have begun to see the lack of basic skills as a critical factor in their ability to create a productive workforce, and many are addressing the problem.

## THE COMMUNITY COLLEGE ROLE

What each generation does affects what other generations can and will do. Our nation now faces a small window of opportunity. A third world is developing within our nation. The gulf between the haves and the have-nots is growing larger. Our once unchallenged preeminence in commerce, industry, science, and technology is being overtaken by competitors from all over the world. So we challenge each community and each community college district to act now—not only for one town, or one college region, but for our nation and its future.

Community colleges have long been recognized as leaders in the literacy movement. This dedication goes beyond mission and results from their philosophy of community building. *Building Communities* stated that "building communities is more than a region to be served, it is a climate to be created" (Commission on the Future of Community Colleges, 1988). Certainly in the field of literacy this has been true. Community colleges have helped their communities understand that they must decide how important a literate population is to their economic health and develop successful strategies. As a result, some communities have taken on the responsibility of solving the literacy puzzle, realizing that learning begins at home and that they must address the problem at the adult and childhood levels. Our blueprint for action is based on local initiative and dedication. It calls for state and federal support in the form of rewards for success and for local collaboration. Its foundation is local responsibility rather than federal solutions because we believe that this is more cost-effective and has a greater possibility of success.

## INITIAL STEPS AT HIGHLAND COMMUNITY COLLEGE

One of the authors came to Highland Community College, Illinois, with many years of experience in adult and continuing education and first-hand contact with those who need quality literacy services. Another came two years ago with literacy program involvement in several states. All came believing that although communities and legislators voice concern for the underprepared, little change has ensued for local programs. Our Highland team realized that if change is to happen, we must take responsibility for its development and implementation. We have created varied and modest efforts that offer some hope to improve funding and services for our adult education and literacy students.

After years of watching state and federal governments struggle to improve funding for literacy and adult education with virtually no local results, we were determined to address it ourselves. In the spring of 1993, we reorganized our workplace program. We put workplace literacy under the direction of the adult education program and determined that whatever profits the group generated would be applied to the total program. Thus far the plan shows promise of yielding impressive results. The curriculum for the workplace is applied to regular classes. Staff training modules can be used for both arms of the program. As we build technology centers around the district, both groups of students benefit. In addition to internal collaboration, the workplace program is generating sufficient income to bolster the total adult education program with operating funds, equipment purchases, and training and development dollars.

We also have come to realize that poor basic skills among adults is one part of a very complex mix of maladies affecting thousands of people within our district. We have worked to build community collaborations that address other family services in two very different target communities—a small rural town and the largest community in our district, population 25,000. The goal is to involve multiple organizations in delivering cooperative programs that focus more on the family and less on agencies.

The smaller community has created its own family literacy project. It is spearheaded by the Kiwanis Club and housed in the senior citizens center, with child care provided by the town's four churches and printing and supplies donated by local merchants. Schools and agencies make referrals into the program, which has operated for two years.

The other community collaboration is still in the formative stages, but it has garnered support from many organizations and agencies to improve results for families and children. The mission statement of Project Collaboration describes its goal: "This is a voluntary group of agencies, institutions and families dedicated to preparing our children for success in life. Through Project Collaboration we are cooperating to assure that our energy resources, skills and commitment are efficiently and systematically coordinated to meet this ultimate goal: That all children in our community will grow up in a strong, healthy family and community environment, meeting their potential and believing in themselves."

Beyond the provision of direct instruction, community colleges' role in supporting literacy efforts has largely been one of advocacy. It is our contention that community colleges can and should do more. We must be leaders in development in effective program development; we must take our needs and concerns to legislators; and to address local needs, we must first secure adequate funding.

We cannot wait for government to solve the problem—we must push government officials to tackle illiteracy in a way that allows local programs to feel the difference, but when the state and federal governments fail to act, we must address funding locally. We must stir our communities to action so that they collaborate to effectively use existing services and find home-grown means of addressing complex needs. But most importantly, community colleges must take the lead. We understand the problem. We have lived it with our students and know that it must be conquered. We know that if we fail, the resulting death spiral will affect every one of us.

*This we know: the Earth does not belong to us, we belong to the Earth. This we know: all things are connected, like the blood which unites one family. All things are connected. Whatever befalls the Earth befalls the sons and daughters of the Earth. We did not weave the web of life; we are merely strands in it. Whatever we do to the web we do to ourselves.*
—Chief Seattle, 1855

*Ruth Mercedes Smith is president of Highland Community College, Illinois. Sandra Feaver is director of adult education at Highland Community College. Vicki Anderson is director of the Learning Assistance Center at Highland Community College.*

## REFERENCES

American Bar Association. *Lawyers for Literacy.* Washington, D.C.: American Bar Association, 1987.

Chisman, F.P. *Jump Start: The Federal Role in Adult Literacy.* Southport, Conn.: Southport Institute for Policy Analysis, 1989

Commission on the Future of Community Colleges. *Building Communities: A Vision for a New Century.* Washington, D.C.: American Association of Community and Junior Colleges, 1988.

Harman, David, and Hunter, Carman St.John. *Adult Illiteracy in the United States.* New York: McGraw-Hill, 1979.

Jenkins, L. et al. *Adult Literacy in America.* Washington, D.C.: U.S. Department of Education, 1993.

Kozol, J. *Illiterate America.* Garden City, New York: Anchor Press/ Doubleday, 1985.

# CHAPTER SIX

# MINORITY RECRUITMENT AT RURAL COLLEGES

## *Julius R. Brown*

Descriptions and definitions of what constitutes a minority are emotion-charged and value-laden. Madeleine F. Green (1990) discusses the sensitivity of the issue with great insight; words develop histories, positive and negative connotations that color the perceptions of readers and listeners. Commonly used terms, though a convenient shorthand, are sometimes inadequate to express the complexities of this issue. We recognize the term "minority" because it aggregates diverse groups, but it does a disservice to African-Americans, Hispanics, native Americans, and Asian-Americans, all included under that umbrella. Words that aggregate can easily lead to stereotypes. Not all minority students are underprepared. Chicanos, Cubans, Puerto Ricans, and Central and South Americans all have different histories and traditions. Some, but not all, Asian-American students outperform their majority counterparts. In short, every group and subgroup is different; it is impossible to generalize about any one group.

Although smaller and/or rural institutions generally have fewer resources for special projects, enrolled minority student populations should equal or exceed the percentage of minorities in the population of each service area. All schools should strive to achieve at least this minimum to be representative of and responsive to their communities.

The definition of "minority" for each college depends on its service area and demographics. In central Alabama where Wallace Community College-Selma (WCCS) is located, there are only two sizable groups: African-American and white. There are very few native Americans, Asians, and Hispanics.

The college is located in an area called the Black Belt. The region got its name when nineteenth-century settlers found that a band of fertile black dirt covered the middle section of Alabama and was particularly well suited to grow cotton. Slaves were brought in and central Alabama became the epitome of the southern plantation society. In some counties blacks outnumbered whites, and the area is still populated by large percentages of African-Americans. The region also suffers from a disproportionately large number of social problems, including low educational attainment, high unemployment and the expected accompanying ills. It is decidedly rural and has a diminishing population.

## Recruitment at Wallace Community College-Selma

At WCCS there is only one program directed exclusively toward minority students—the minority math and science program. All other efforts occur within normal recruitment or recruitment of the disadvantaged. By focusing on the disadvantaged, the college makes significant inroads to the minority population while serving residents from the majority. WCCS creates an image and reality that all students are welcome. This is done by making sure all publications are racially and ethnically representative of the areas's population.

The college makes sure that recruitment outreach goes to all feeder schools and establishes a rapport with them. In a rural setting it is often necessary to provide transportation for students to get to campus or participate in cultural and educational events. Links with groups such as adult education agencies, human services offices, state employment offices, and other training organizations ensure access to minorities.

*TRIO.* WCCS is fortunate to house two of the U.S. Department of Education's TRIO Programs, Student Support Services and Talent Search. Student Services is designed to aid disadvantaged students from initial enrollment to graduation. The program provides developmental instruction, tutoring, and counseling. Two years ago WCCS added a transfer coordinator, who helps transfer-track students gain admission to other institutions upon graduation from WCCS. In its second year of operation, the effort gained $137,000 in transfer funds for WCCS graduates. The coordinator obtained much of it by seeking out transfer funds and taking graduating students to prospective four-year transfer institutions. Overall, Student Support Services serves about 260 students from the general college population.

WCCS received funding for Talent Search in the summer of 1990. This program is designed to assist disadvantaged sixth- through twelfth-graders with the potential to succeed and go to college. It is considered a life-altering program and has a major impact in WCC's service area. WCCS counselors assigned to six high schools and five junior high schools provide counseling, tutoring, special classes, and education programs. WCCS teams work with local school districts to supplement and enrich the secondary program. Each year the program serves over 800 students, and there is a waiting list.

*New Beginnings for Women.* This federally funded program is designed to assist displaced homemakers. It provides counseling, advising, some tuition grants, and, most importantly, advocacy. Whether the student's goal is immediate employment or further education, the program counselor helps the student achieve her goal. WCCS employs a counselor who makes program students aware of college resources and opportunities. The counselor provides support ranging from employment interviewing techniques to assistance in gaining program admission. One of the most popular and positive program areas is the health care field. The program serves about 100 students per year.

*Minority Math and Science Program.* This program is designed to further the education of minority high achievers and encourage them to consider careers in math and science. For consideration, graduating high school students have to be in the top quartile of the graduating class or have at least a 3.0 GPA in a college prep curriculum. Selected students are given a summer experience at historically black Alabama A&M University in Huntsville, where they take classes and intern at organizations like NASA, Intergraph, United Technology, and Teledyne. In the fall, the students return to WCCS to gain their associate degrees. Two cycles were started, and the vast majority of the first group have graduated and won transfer scholarships to four-year schools. The first cycle had fifteen students and the second had seven. Funding is being sought to start a third cycle.

*Adult Education Cluster.* At WCCS, adult education is approached creatively. All of it is geared to promote basic educational competency and encourage further education at WCCS or other schools if the student desires to continue. There are six approaches to adult education at the college:

- *Adult Education Classes.* Specific courses based on each learner's skill level are provided at 27 locations by paid professional staff and a large group of volunteers.
- *GED Preparation and Testing.* The college provides standard GED preparation to 1,000 students at adult education facilities. The instruction is free to students and is part of the state's effort to enhance adult education attainment.
- *Literacy Van.* This joint project of the Selma/Dallas County Library and WCCS brings books and teaching to remote areas of Dallas County. The library provides the van and materials and WCCS provides the instructor. The college provides an assistant to care for dependent children as mothers gain on-site instruction. While a larger number of contacts are made annually, the library and college pick twelve families and attempt to bring about significant improvements. Van graduates are assisted in finding funds to continue their education. The first graduate obtained a GED and received a WCCS scholarship. Unlike in urban areas, where transportation is available, these students would not have been served were it not for the van.
- *Telephone Tutoring.* A skilled adult education instructor has a toll-free phone line and interacts individually with students. Exchange of materials occurs by mail. The service is free to students and about seventy people are served annually. Increasingly the service is being used by employed people who feel a need to improve their basic education. Some of these have changing shifts or obligations that make this service their only option.
- *JOBS.* Recent federal regulations make involvement in some form of training or education mandatory for welfare recipients. The

JOBS program has provided funding to WCCS for its adult education program. Three teaching units with a total capacity of sixty students have been granted to the college. These students are treated as any others in WCCS programs. However, special transportation arrangements, a rural necessity, had to be made to ensure program participation.
- *Homeless Program.* WCCS is funded to provide educational and life-skill training for about eighty-nine local homeless people.

*Tech Prep.* The Tech Prep concept, which marries high schools and community colleges through articulated programs, enhances the enrollment of all students. Every effort is made to ensure that minorities are included in this dramatic instructional change.

*Academic Competition for Excellence (ACE).* About 45 area schools—black and white, rich and poor, public and private—are invited to participate in this competition. Advance assistance is given to any school that needs it. In the Black Belt, public school participation ensures minority involvement. Despite the large number of schools, only about 1,000 students participate, due to the sparsely populated nature of rural areas.

## CENTRAL VIRGINIA COMMUNITY COLLEGE

The following programs have been implemented at Central Virginia Community College (CVCC), where Belle Wheelan, a member of the Rural/Community College Commission, is president.

*Alliance for Excellence.* This outreach effort is designed to work in partnership with local black churches through an advisory committee of ministers and lay people. Programs and seminars on relevant topics have been presented to adult, young adult, and teenage individuals. Topics have included planning for colleges, obtaining financial aid, motivation, self-esteem, and the black family.

*Cooperative Efforts with Area Schools.* This program connects the college with Lynchburg-area schools. Special presentations are made to various groups and classes. Follow-up contacts are made in person and with letters and phone calls. Groups are invited to campus for tours. The college has been involved with Focus, a special project designed to acquaint selected students with higher education. Subjects presented to the students include career exploration, college selection, and self-esteem.

*Adult Outreach.* Programs are presented through the inner-city YWCA. Inner-city residents have been contacted and encouraged to attend CVCC.

## Concluding Thoughts

Why is minority recruitment important? Out of enlightened self-interest, it's important that every American citizen be as developed and capable as possible for the United States to compete globally for favorable trade and quality of life. The country can ill afford not to use every available mind and body positively. The alternatives of crime, violence, poverty, and social rebellion already place an intolerable burden on our society. Unless these problems are addressed, major consequences for the American way of life will result. In a more narrow educational sense, Madeleine Green provides a compelling declarative statement on the need for minority recruitment:

Recruiting and retaining minority undergraduates are essential to ensuring equity for minority citizens and to improving the learning environment for all students. A college degree provides increased employment opportunity, as well as enhanced social standing. Anything less than full access for all citizens to this important credential is clearly unjust. Equally important is the impact of a homogeneous campus on all students; an educational experience that does not reflect the pluralism of our country and the importance of minority individuals and cultures is simply deficient (p. 29).

Does a commitment to diversity mean the reduction of quality? The answer to the question is an unequivocal no. Not maintaining or stressing quality is perhaps the cruelest joke of all. All students must be held to high standards and be educated to become productive contributors to society. The nation needs their skills and abilities. The real question is whether institutions will take steps toward or invest resources in enhancing minority achievement while pursuing quality. Again, Green states it well:

The commitment to provide quality education for minorities must be constantly reaffirmed at all levels of an institution. Similarly, each program and service plays a role in enhancing diversity. Active participation by all is necessary to make a commitment to quality and diversity which are central to the mission of the college. Those in top leadership positions, however, must establish a climate that will support the specific activities that translate commitment into results (p. 166).

*Julius R. Brown is president of Wallace Community College-Selma, Alabama.*

## REFERENCES

Green, Madeleine F. *Minorities on Campus: A Handbook for Enhancing Diversity.* American Council on Education. Washington, D.C. 1990.

# CHAPTER SEVEN

# EXTERNAL FUND DEVELOPMENT: THE GOLD MEDAL

## *Paul Alcantra*

The interest of the American sports fan is captured every two years when the media bombards us with every facet of the Olympic Games. It is clear in the athlete's mind and in the spectator's enthusiasm that only one outcome represents the dream fulfilled—the gold medal. With it comes immediate stardom, world recognition, and in many cases financial wealth. One emerging trend in the management and leadership of community colleges—referred to by Deegan (1989) as the "fourth concept of management and leadership"—is entrepreneurship. Entrepreneurship, in the form of fundraising, is playing a major role in the success of many community colleges, and more and more are catching the fever to go for the gold.

As state and local funding dwindle, demographics change, competition for students increases, and demand for scholarships and financial aid grows, many community colleges have joined the game by increasing efforts to raise funds from the private sector. As Reinhard (1993) noted, fundraising was once almost exclusively the domain of four-year institutions, but more community colleges are joining with their foundations and development offices to solicit significant donations from alumni and corporations through capital campaigns and major fundraising events. Twenty community colleges raised more than one million dollars in fiscal 1992, nearly twice the number in 1990 (Reinhard, 1993).

As Deegan points out, most of what happened in community colleges over the past three decades involved a period of growth, when bigger was equated with better. New colleges and multicampus districts emerged, funding changed, and organizational units within colleges grew. Most of this resulted from governance and management models that combined collegiate, political, and bureaucratic elements.

During the past few years, primarily because of fiscal and demographic circumstances and taxpayer revolts, interest has grown in using entrepreneurship to supplement traditional community college approaches to solving problems and creating opportunities. Entrepreneurial activities are defined as those that help generate resources, such as creating private fundraisraising foundations. Several emerging issues will make entrepreneurship a dominant management concept in this decade. Deegan (1989) outlines some of the issues: increasing competition for students and faculty among all segments of higher education, the need to fund and manage developing technology, changing student clientele, worsening faculty shortages, growing state and federal legislation and guidelines, and more management of colleges and universities by new state agencies. These and other issues will challenge management to be more creative and more effective.

Demands for additional social services provided by community colleges, the needs of a changing student clientele, and competition from other providers may require more entrepreneurial management strategies. Someone in the top levels of each administration must provide support and guidance for entrepreneurial initiatives to break down barriers and ensure a fair chance for new ventures. The official most frequently in administrative control of a foundation is the president of the college or a separate foundation director.

Recent studies indicate a growing trend among community colleges toward creating foundations geared toward raising funds. Success and use of foundations will vary depending on the history, traditions, and financial status of each institution and the commitment of its chief executive officer. Entrepreneurship and its potential successes require strategic planning, an active search for opportunities, a venture capital fund, long-term emphasis, and systematic evaluation. External ventures need: goals for one year, three years, five years, and longer; quality control; a realistic sense of potentials and limits; numerous volunteers; and the commitment of all groups within the institution.

Community colleges can learn a major lesson from the perspective of the marketplace: "Trying to raise money on the basis of an organization's needs will work just about as well as trying to obtain a bank loan by pleading poverty. Too many institutions still haven't accepted this reality. They continue to believe that the more desperate for funds they appear, the more successful at fund-aising they'll be. But donors are tired of hearing these pleas over and over again. In fact, from the viewpoint of the donor, an organization has no needs" (Lord, 1983). Taxpayers could be said to hold the same viewpoint as donors.

According to Lord, "the days of hand-wringing and arm-twisting are drawing to a close" (1983, p. 5). Today, a successful fundraiser invites people to invest in a worthy enterprise. "The focus is less on donations per se and more on the development of donors and institutions." The essentials of raising money are "about people, how they feel, how they think and act, and what happens between them when they're engaged in the enterprise of philanthropy" (Lord, 1983, p. vii).

Successful college organizations today are putting philanthropic dollars to work in meeting people's needs. They address the community's potential and society's aspirations. They address opportunities and show how the institution is poised to capitalize on these opportunities, on behalf of all those it serves.

## CCCC Experience

The current fundraising effort of Cerro Coso Community College (CCCC), California, exemplifies the qualities of a successful organization addressing opportunities and working to meet the people's needs. In 1989 several leaders in Mammoth Lakes, California, founded the Mammoth Lakes Foundation in order to establish a college in the town. The effort was spearheaded by Mammoth Mountain Ski Area founder Dave McCoy, who contributed his commitment to developing higher education and the arts in the eastern Sierra Nevadas, his personal financial support, and in-kind ski area services. In 1990 the foundation financed leased facilities and equipment to provide access to classes. In 1991, the foundation board employed a full-time executive director and since then has gone full speed ahead.

On October 27, 1993, the "College in Mammoth" effort made two major announcements. A draft master plan for development of a new college was unveiled, and the foundation initiated a year-long donation drive through Snowcreek Fairway Condominium to benefit the college fund. All proceeds from the drive will go to the foundation. Part of the condominium was donated by Dempsey Construction, a local firm. Escrow services were donated by Chicago Title. John Robinson, regional director for the Southern California Edison Company, co-chaired the Eastern Sierra College Committee and played a major role in acquiring a 255-acre land donation from Edison. "This is a terrific example of a community coming together to realize a shared dream. Initial reaction has been tremendous. People are very enthusiastic about buying and helping sell the tickets. It's a good feeling—this is going to be a significant contribution to the college effort," said Robinson.

The campus center plan presents a multiuse concept on land the foundation intends to acquire from the U.S. Forest Service through a land exchange, made possible by Edison's donation. The intended campus site is within the town of Mammoth Lakes. Evan Russell, the ski area's marketing director and spokesperson for the foundation's Strategic Planning Committee, indicated that the master plan was a ten-to-fifteen-year multicampus commitment. It is sensitive to the environment and meets community needs through public input. The foundation expects to establish a cultural center, an outdoor amphitheater, four-year college facilities, and student housing. This example of a foundation's dream focuses on people, development of donors, communty needs, and creating the institution.

Too many colleges portray themselves as needy organizations rather than providers of promising programs. Seymour (1988) makes it vividly clear that donors give to winners. He suggests that the case for giving must be bigger than the institution. It must be presented in a way that catches the eye, warms the heart, and stirs the mind.

A college can tap into a variety of financial support sources. The four major donor markets are: individuals, foundations, corporations, and government. Individuals account for 83 percent of charitable gifts. Why do individuals give to charity? Nonprofit organizations need to understand these motives to conduct effective fundraising. The best working hypothesis is that individuals give in order to get something back. Givers expect the organization to use the money efficiently and the fundraiser to show gratitude.

Marketing is a subject of growing interest to non-profit organizations. Kotler (1982) implies that marketing is more than the using personal selling, advertising, and publicity to create and maintain demand. Marketing is knowing how to plan and manage the organization's exchange relations with various segments of the public. "Marketing is the analysis, planning, implementation, and control of carefully formulated programs designed to bring about voluntary exchanges of values with target markets for the purpose of achieving organizational objectives" (Kotler, 1982).

According to Lord, "any society needs healthy business and government sectors. We have now come to realize that in order to advance our civilization, we need a healthy nonprofit sector" (1983, p. iii). Community colleges have further to go than many four-year institutions; however, interest in fundraising at two-year institutions appears to be at record levels. Out of necessity and as a result of declining resources, community colleges need help from the private sector. We need to be in the games to go for the gold.

*Paul Alcantra is dean of the Eastern Sierra College Center at Cerro Coso Community College, California.*

## REFERENCES

Deegan, William L. "Entrepreneurial Management." In Terry O'Banion (Ed.), *Innovation in the Community College.* New York: American Association of Community and Junior Colleges/American Council of Education/Macmillian, 1989.

Kotler, Philip. *Marketing for Non-Profit Organizations.* Second Edition. Englewood Cliffs, N.J.: Prentice-Hall, 1982.

Lick, Michael F., and Tolle, Donald J. *Community College Development: Alternative Fund Raising Strategies.* Indianapolis: R & R Newkirk, 1978.

Lord, James Gregory. *The Raising of Money: Thirty-Five Essentials Every Trustee Should Know.* Cleveland: Third Sector Press, 1983.

Reinhard, Bill. "A Capitol Jackpot." *Community College Times,* September 7, 1993, 5 (17), 1, 10.

Seymour, Harold J. *Designs for Fund-Raising: Principles, Patterns, Techniques.* 2nd edition. Rockville, Md.: Fund-Raising Institute, 1988.

# CHAPTER EIGHT

# EVIDENCING EFFECTIVENESS

## W.A. Griffin, Jr.

Small and rural community colleges are being asked to do more things for more people with fewer resources. Business wants this and that, students want new and better services, special interest groups in the community want certain programs, and boards of trustees want to hold the line on taxes. Everyone, it seems, has an agenda, and the college's faculty, staff, and administration are caught in the middle.

Today, more than ever, these colleges must set real missions that are less global and more in tune with their communities' real needs. They do not and never will have enough resources to provide for every societal niche. It is extremely important that they choose which niches to develop services for and market services to. Most colleges have not done so; unless they do, they will become weaker and unable to provide quality. "Most community colleges have not organized to address change and create preferred futures. Many have not organized to gather environmental intelligence needed to provide strategic advantage in the next decade" (Lorenzo and Banach, 1990, p. 19).

Colleges that have not addressed change and thought about preferred futures are not sure which niche to be in, or worse, see every niche as an opportunity that must be accepted. Colleges in these situations will likely be unresponsive to change or student needs. They will always go with the status quo and are always prepared to defend it. They lack direction and cannot plan for the future.

Gone are the days of large enrollment increases. Across the country public perceptions are changing about what colleges do and should be doing. Small and rural colleges will have to demonstrate, in ways that the public can understand, the quality they provide. "In this new age, community colleges will have to define and document student success. Most are not prepared to accommodate either task very well because their measurement systems have been attuned only to indicators of quantity" (Lorenzo and Banach, 1991, p. 7).

With all the challenges come opportunities. Whether a small or rural college has defined niches relates to its mission statement. This in turn relates to policy and vision. Colleges cannot be all things to all people. Vision, policy, and mission statements can provide solutions to the issues of institutional niches and create advantages in serving target markets with quality services.

## THE MPCCA EXPERIENCE

The Mid-Plains Community College Area serves eighteen rural counties in west and central Nebraska. The service area reaches from the Kansas border on the south to the South Dakota border on the north. Slightly fewer than 100,000 residents live in this rural and isolated section and no other postsecondary institutions operate there except through distance learning and some offerings on our campuses through the University of Nebraska at Kearney. MPCCA's history has been one of attempting to serve every need of the service area.

In 1991 a North Central Association of Colleges and Schools (NCACS) accreditation team visited the college. The accreditation team made several recommendations and planned to revisit the college in 1995. MPCCA was forced to look at niches to see where it fits. After NCACS formally granted continued accreditation early in 1992, the area chancellor prompted the creation of several groups, monitoring and guiding efforts where products were directly related to addressing NCACS's concerns. Among those groups were the following:

- An ad hoc Mission Statement Review Committee was formed early in 1993 and held its first meeting April 2. Chaired by the chancellor, it continued its efforts until completing its task in the fall of 1993.
- An area-wide Planning Council chaired by McCook Community College's campus president recommended the hiring of an

outside consultant who would guide and facilitate MPCCA strategic planning. After MPCCA governing board approval, the consultant was hired and a comprehensive area-wide strategic planning process began in May 1992 and continues to the present day.
- In April 1992 a Task Force on Assessment was created to develop an area-wide plan to assess and document student academic achievement.
- In October 1993 the MPCCA chancellor formally established a Focused Group Task Force to oversee institutional preparations for the visit and to guide, review, and adjust a report.

The NCA focus visit has forced MPCCA to review some of its basic philosophies and assumptions, by addressing its role and mission statement, implementing a strategic planning process, and recognizing the need for a systemwide plan to assess student academic achievement. These three concerns have forced the college to begin finding its niches and start the process of evidencing effectiveness.

## ROLE AND MISSION

The 1991 NCA report requests that the MPCAA revise its mission statement to "address all major institutional functions and activities consistent with Nebraska statues; articulate predominant institutional values; and be of sufficient scope to provide necessary flexibility, yet specific enough to serve as a guide to planning, decision making and assessment" (MPCCA Mission Statement, 1993). The task force established by the chancellor met several times to review the current statement, looking at Nebraska statutes and working on the draft. After several months the draft was given to the chancellor, who then sent it to every faculty, staff, and administration member for comments. These were considered and a revised draft was sent to selected members of the community. Their comments were reviewed and another revision was sent to the Board of Governors for approval. The approved mission statement reads:

The mission of Mid-Plains Community College Area is educating students. To that end, the Area is committed to excellence in educational programming. In order to facilitate and enhance quality educational experiences in a constantly changing environment, the Area is dedicated to continuous improvement (1993).

The new statement meets all the requirements of Nebraska law and the NCA. The document also details the role, the scope, and seven institutional goals of the college. It has greatly encouraged the college to focus on niches.

## STRATEGIC PLAN

The MPCCA strategic plan is a living document that continues to evolve. The plan is divided into three major areas: instructional service goals, student support service goals, and institutional support goals. These allow for major and minor goals in areas we know fit our niches. For example, under instructional service goals are academic transfer, vocational-technical, and community service goals. These in turn have subgoals; for example, academic transfer subgoals include general education core, remedial and developmental education, and distance education. By setting these goals and subgoals based on niches, the college can evidence effectiveness.

## ASSESSMENT PLAN

MPCCA was cited by the NCA team for not having the means to assess student achievement. From 1991 to the present the college has been through numerous exercises to determine steps for assessing student academic achievement, student services/student development, educational program quality, faculty accomplishments, institutional research, quantity and quality service to the area, enhancement of resources, and institutional climate.

The college's assessment task force is another instrument used to determine niches and will lead to evidencing effectiveness. As MPCCA continues to implement the work of the task force, the results will lead to institutional effectiveness through assessment.

## CONCLUSION

The small and/or rural community college must be concerned about evidencing effectiveness. MPCCA is well on its way to determining its unique niches as a direct result of the review and rewriting of its mission statement, the development of the strategic plan, and the creation of valid means of assessment.

*W.A. Griffin, Jr. is president of the McDonald-Belton Campus of Mid-Plains Community College, Nebraska.*

## REFERENCES

Lorenzo, Albert L., and Banach, William J. *The Top Ten Issues Facing America's Community Colleges.* Warren, Mich.: Macomb Community College Institute for Future Studies, 1990.

Lorenzo, Albert L., and Banach, William J. *The Top Ten Issues Facing America's Community Colleges, 1991 Edition.* Warren, Mich.: Macomb Community College Institute for Future Studies, 1991.

*MPCCA Mission Statement,* Mid-Plains Community College Area, October 1993.